Peace
by
Piece

from the heart and hands
of a quilter

Naomi Pearson

National Library of Canada Cataloguing in Publication

Pearson, Naomi 1954 -
   Peace by Piece/Naomi Pearson

ISBN 0-9735517-3-9

PS8631.E33P43 2005 C811L6 C2005-904522-1

Cover - original quilt block by Naomi Pearson
Cover graphics by Pat Kielbach,
Frogbelly Printing and Promotions, Drayton Valley, Alberta

Printed by Swarm Enterprises, Edmonton

Published by GRASSROOTS PUBLISHING
Lillian Ross, Publisher
Box 7834, Drayton Valley, Alberta T7A 1S9

To my husband, Howard,
my children, Julie and Kurt,
you are my heart.

To my friends at
the Hearts and Hands Quilt Guild
in Drayton Valley,
you are hands with heart!

To my God,
You are the Peace of the pieces.

Introduction

When I began penning these little poems, they were a creative way to laugh with my Wednesday quilting friends about some of the quirks that are so unique to quilters. As I began to write, it became much more. I thought of the role the simple quilt has played to express love, warm hearts (and feet) and the joy that each stitch brings. I never realized how much is stitched into each gift.

The creative avenue of fabric and heart have made it a craft that I hope to pursue for many years (and have access to enough stash to have no problem doing that very thing).

My mother and mother-in-law have blessed our family with warmth and love as they have provided all of the coverings for the beds in our home. Our children loved their baby quilts to death and treasure the ones received for graduation.

The stories contained in the poetry in this book are not real life events but based on the experiences of friends and family. Maybe you will catch a glimpse of yourself. In most cases, the quilts are fictional.

Laugh with me and cry with me as we look at life through a quilter's eyes. May you find peace from the Maker of the pieces.

5

Naomi Pearson

Peace by Piece

A quilt
fabric as a whole
divided
to make a kaleidoscope
of pattern
formed by the designer
to create an object of beauty
piece by piece

a life
though whole
divided
happiness and sadness
failure and success
laughter and tears
patterns in part
formed by the designer
to create a person of beauty
peace by piece

Table of Contents

from my heart

from the hands with heart

from the Peace of the pieces

from
the
heart

Naomi Pearson

✠ Chosen Gifts ✠

Oh, I can't cook and I can't sew,
       Where was my mother's head?
The only thing she gave to me
       Was a rag quilt on my bed.

My chequebook does not balance.
       My plants just do not live.
Why couldn't Mom plan better
       Of the gifts she had to give?

My brother spent his Saturdays
       and Sundays with my dad.
With wrenches, sockets, nuts and bolts,
       they toiled in our garage.
Dad changed our oil, rotated tires,
       made sure our cars would run.
Now the things he learned from Gramps,
       he's passed on to his son.

10

My brother bought an old Ford truck,
       I thought it was a wreck.
With bondo and a can of paint
       with red metallic fleck,
My dad and brother worked on sanding,
       smoothing to the core.
My brother drove that sharp red truck
       'til he was twenty-four!

My brother, he can build a house
       or make a picture frame.
He learned from Dad, who learned from his,
       and they mastered the trade.
A hammer in his hand or even
       just a saw or drill,
From Dad he watched, and out of that,
       he learned a useful skill.

But, I can't cook and I can't sew,
Where was my mother's head?
The only thing she gave to me
Was a rag quilt on my bed.

My chequebook does not balance.
My plants just do not live.
Why couldn't Mom plan better
Of the gifts she had to give?

My friend, she stopped the other day,
a hurting heart to share.
She thanked me for my listening ear
and for my loving care.
I wrapped her in my quilt and poured
hot chocolate in her mug.
She smiled at me, she snuggled in
and thanked me for the hug.

12

I didn't understand, for from me
        no hug had been given.
But she explained that my rag quilt
        seemed like a touch from heaven.
She thanked me for my generous heart,
        my laughter quick and free,
And I began to see the gifts
        that Mom had given me.

Friends came first in our household
        before the dust and dishes.
Mom listened to their hopes and dreams
        and even shattered wishes.
Her easy laughter made you feel
        that there was always hope,
When the burdens of this life just seemed
        that you would never cope.

13

She made me practise keyboard first
        as each new day would start.
She showed me when you sang,
        you always did so from your heart.
She taught me how to live for God,
        how through Him I am free.
She demonstrated, when in pain,
        find possibility.

No, I can't cook and I can't sew,
        I'll learn from books instead.
For my mom sent a needed hug
        In the rag quilt on my bed.

My chequebook does not balance,
        My plants, they do not live.
But I thank God for my mom
        And the gifts she chose to give.

Inspired by my daughter, Julie,
who once told me that the greatest compliment
she had ever received
was that
"she was just like her mom."
Julie is an accomplished musician,
loves to try new recipes,
and is planting her first garden this spring.
She does not sew.

Naomi Pearson

▦ Coordinated ▦

My home, it is the kind you see
　　　　in women's magazines.
　　　　　　　　My draperies coordinate
　　　　　　　　　　　　in subtle shades of green.
My cushions match the pictures,
　　　　the candles match the floor,
　　　　　　　　upon which lays a cayenne rug,
　　　　　　　　　　　completing my décor.

Imagine to my horror,
　　　　a gift I did receive,
　　　　　　　　a patchwork quilt from Mother,
　　　　　　　　　　　with colours red and green,
Yellow, turquoise, purple,
　　　　orange, olive and bright blue,
　　　　　　　　every imaginable colour
　　　　　　　　　　　in every shade and hue.

16

I could not put this in my room,
  the colours did not go!
    What was Mother thinking
      as she stitched each crooked row?
I picked it up to take upstairs
  to find a place to hide,
    when a patch of yellow fabric
      on the corner caught my eye.

An Easter dress, with daisy chains,
  that Mom had made for me.
    We matched that day her dress and mine,
      I smiled in memory.
Why, that bright blue was from a blouse
  she'd fashioned with great care,
    to match my skirt and bobby socks
      and ribbons for my hair.

Naomi Pearson

The pink and purple calico
        warmed my churning heart,
                Mom had made that dress to wear
                        the day that school would start.
I searched and sure enough
        a paisley print of red and green,
                had been a special Christmas dress,
                        I'd felt just like a queen.

There was the plaid of orange and gold,
        the skirt she sewn for me.
                She thought that mini was way too short,
                        eight inches above my knee!
It matched the cutest little shirt
        and fashion sense knew better,
                then I found the fuchsia pink
                        she'd made into a sweater.

18

The jacket from my baseball gang
            in the ugliest shade of green,
                        but Mom had made one faithfully
                                    for each one on the team.
The powder blue from my first date,
            with matching floral swirls,
                        my outfits never looked homemade,
                                    were the envy of the girls.

The turquoise blue Hawaiian print
            was for school luau days.
                        The tie-dye psychedelic pink
                                    was from the hippy phase.
Soft yellow from a ribboned gown,
            roses wound their way,
                        with matching shoes and jewelry
                        for graduation day.

Naomi Pearson

The satin and imported lace,
    beads stitched side by side,
        here were pieces from the day
            that I'd become a bride.
I looked again at the colourful quilt
    that I had shunned so fast.
        Mom had stitched a memory
            from the colours of my past.

My home is still set in décor
    of cayenne, butter and sage.
        The patchwork quilt from Mother
            now is proudly on display.
I've learned from Mom, my children,
    my friends and God above,
        A matching home is nothing
            if it's not wrapped up in love.

Thank you, Mom, for a wardrobe built with love.

20

My mother, my friend.

Naomi Pearson

❄ Gramma's Quilt ❄

You don't remember Gramma,
She died in '75.
She left for you a special quilt
The day that you'd arrive.

It had colours of the sunshine,
As she stitched she'd pray,
That God would give you sunny days
Amidst the ones of grey.

It had colours of the rainbow,
As she stitched she'd pray,
That you would see God's promises
And claim them each new day.

It had colours of the raging seas,
As she stitched she'd pray,
That as you faced the storms in life
Her God would guide your way.

It had colours of the sunrise.
She'd prayed a blessing you would be,
To those whose lives you wound around,
God's love in you they'd see.

She prayed you'd have a caring heart,
A listening ear, and play a part,
In lives changed through your gift of love,
For a faith in God above.

You came to us not long ago,
We wrapped you in Gram's quilt,
With eyes like Dad, a smile like Mom's
And skin as soft as silk.

We watched you grow and use Gram's quilt
For such creative things,
One day a cape for superman,
One day for angel wings.

Naomi Pearson

One day to build a house for tea,
One day to hug beside,
One day to keep you from the cold,
One day a veiled bride.

We watched you grow into the girl,
For whom Gramma had prayed.
Your faith in God, your caring heart,
Laughter admidst your pain.

We never would have chosen,
The path He gave to you.
Today we wrap you in your quilt,
Your short life here is through.

Today when you see Gramma,
I know she'll meet you there.
Thank her for the quilt she made,
And for her faithful prayers.

Although I have never lost a child, I ache for those who have.
Gramma Pearson is still with us and has faithfully prayed for each
of her children,grandchildren, and great-grandchildren..
They each have a special quilt on their bed.

24

*Mom Pearson, a Godly mom,
grandmother and great grandmother*

❖ Kite Quilt ❖

Read a story,
Catch a ball,
Make a kite to fly.
For all too soon you turn
around,
And childhood has passed by.

⊞ My Quilt of Memories ⊞

I guard against the winter chill,
     'neath my quilt of memory,
Printed pictures, woven patterns,
     thoughts of you and me.

The laughter in your eyes,
     as you held me in your arms,
I was too young to realize
     the power of my charm.

You chased me in the lake,
     you threw me in the air.
First days of school you held me tight,
     and prayed a little prayer.

You taught me how to ride a bike,
     and how to catch and pitch.
You didn't scold me when I drove
     our car into the ditch.

You walked me down the aisle the day,
that I became a bride.
When asked, "Who gives this girl?"
you whispered, "Her mom and I."

You paced the floor when I was sick,
sat by and held my hand.
You taught me God was always good,
when I didn't understand.

I close my eyes and see the way
you always looked at Mom.
There never was a cause to doubt,
she was your chosen one.

You drove across the mountains,
to simply share our joy,
As we added to our family,
a little girl and boy.

You patiently would listen,
   as they chattered off your ear.
They were your pride and joy,
   too quickly went the years.

I run my hand across the quilt,
   and the memories we've had.
I wish I'd said I love you more.
   I really miss you, Dad.

Wilfred Klaiber
1914 - 1999

29

Naomi Pearson

 No More

No more crumpled quilt
there upon the floor.
No more clothes piled
from dresser to the door.

No more winter coats
rolled up into a ball.
No more guitars lining
walls along the hall.

No more dishes that didn't
make it to the sink.
No more problems
that solving makes me think.

No more pleading to
turn the music down.
My car's now in the driveway
when I need to go to town.

No more impatient
waiting for the phone.
Our empty nest has come.
Our youngest has left home.

No more hurtful conflicts,
but now I think I see,
The reason we didn't see eye-to-eye,
is he is just like me.

He doesn't look back and stretches out
his wings with which to soar.
I wave goodbye and turn to enter
the new world of 'no more'.

No more midnight talks to help me
see into his heart.
No more help with chores that have always
been his part.

No more riotous laughter as he plans
his latest scheme.
No more dreamy poring over
snowboard magazines.

No more "Mom, come here,
you've got to hear this latest tune."
No more "Let's have lunch today,
I'll pick you up at noon."

No more twinkle as he meets
a special friend.
No more childhood fantasies,
for they have reached their end.

You give them roots, then give them wings,
as the years you carefully plan.
I'm not sure you're ever prepared
for your baby to be a man.

I sometimes long a little,
for the things that are no more.
I miss the laughter and occasionally,
the quilt upon the floor.

Kurt, my baby boy!

33

Naomi Pearson

🖼 Summer's Lament 🖼

Oh the summer's lament:
There is no time to sew.
There's fencing, seeding, weeding,
And there's always lawn to mow.

> *The summer's lament,*
> *I love to see things grow,*
> *But all these needs outside my house*
> *Leave little time to sew.*

I looked outside and watched
The yellow dandelions grow.
The weeds were getting higher
And the lawn needed a mow.

> I put on my blue jeans,
> A sleeveless shirt, and runners too.
> Maybe I could mow the lawn
> And get to sew by noon.

I got out my red Roper,
Filled it to the top with gas.
I watched my acre lawn get
Neat and trim with every pass.

> Round and round I went,
> The time seemed to go oh, so slow.
> What good's a riding mower
> If it has no get and go?

Oh the summer's lament:
There is no time to sew.
There's fencing, seeding, weeding,
And there's always lawn to mow.

> *The summer's lament,*
> *I love to see things grow,*
> *But all these needs outside my house*
> *Leave little time to sew.*

35

Naomi Pearson

I looked down at the gears and saw
That I had chosen third.
Maybe five is faster,
I'm sure that's what I've heard.

      I moved to fifth, gas to fast,
      Made sure no brake was on.
      I popped the clutch and catwalked
      That lawn mower cross the lawn.

Back in third I chose to drive
With much more common sense.
Daydreaming of my sewing room,
I ran into the fence.

      I backed up looking right and left,
      Taking it real slow.
      Too late, I saw the pieces
      Of our brand new garden hose.

Oh the summer's lament:
There is no time to sew
There's fencing, seeding, weeding,
And there's always lawn to mow.

> *The summer's lament,*
> *I love to see things grow,*
> *But all these needs outside my house*
> *Leave little time to sew.*

Now the sun was beaming down,
Already two o'clock.
I have to get this mowing done,
Though it is way too hot.

> I looked both ways and lifted off
> My sleeveless shirt with ease.
> I tied it round my waist,
> My ample bosom caught the breeze.

37

My husband called me later on
And said he'd be delayed.
He'd heard the funniest story
At the coffee shop today.

An operator checking wells
Was dead sure that he saw,
A lady flying on a riding mower
In the raw!

Oh the summer's lament:
There is no time to sew
There's fencing, seeding, weeding,
And there's always lawn to mow.

The summer's lament,
I love to see things grow,
But all these needs outside my house
Leave little time to sew.

❧ The Best Laid Plans ❧

I've been feeling a bit guilty
    as my Wednesdays are consumed,
With sewing, coffee, treats and lunch
    at our quilt guild sewing room.

My husband is putting up a front,
    pretends it's no big deal,
But I know the disappointment
    when he thinks of the evening meal.

He enjoys to end his day
    with the smell of fresh baked bread,
Of supper in the oven,
    the assurance he'll be fed.

I guess that's not too much to ask,
    but Wednesday's such a treat.
I'm too busy with my sewing
    to plan what we should eat!

One day, late spring,
　　　　the last Wednesday in June,
I decided to surprise him.
　　　　I left the guild at noon.

I'd taken out that morning,
　　　　a roast, a fine prime rib.
I came home to make the finest meal
　　　　a wife could ever give.

I baked fresh buns with whole wheat flour,
　　　　and then I baked a pie,
Banana cream, his favorite,
　　　　he was just going to die!

I double stuffed potatoes,
　　　　creamed carrots with the peas,
Then I whipped up Yorkshires,
　　　　I knew he would be pleased.

China that we never use,
        the special crystal bowl,
I polished up the silverware.
        I was on a roll!

I lit the candles, dimmed the lights,
        "Why not make his day?"
I spritzed perfume, recombed my hair
        and donned a negligee.

I waited....... and I waited.....
        for my man to come.
The roast that had been medium rare
        was now beyond well done.

The Yorkshire was all wrinkled,
        the gravy had a skin.
The potatoes had a crust,
        and I won't say my thoughts of him!

41

Wait! Maybe he's been hurt
        or by an accident delayed!
The more I thought, the more I worried,
        I became dismayed.

Oh silly me, I realized,
        I'll call him on his phone.
He answered and I sweetly asked him
        just when he'd be home!

"Won't be late, just shootin' the breeze
        while leanin' on the rail.
The boys and I are looking at steeds
        at the Rocky Auction sale!"

"Have a good day with the girls?
        Read that thing I wrote?"
I slammed that old receiver down....
        and then I saw the note.

Hi Hon, it's Wednesday morning
           and you'll be at the guild.
I'm so proud of you, you're doing great
           with all those quilts you build.

It's horse sale night so I guess, of course,
           you know where I will be.
Here's twenty bucks, take a friend,
           and have supper out on me!

My anger turned to sheepishness,
           though the meal was a wreck,
I put away thoughts of spitefulness
           and the high necked flannelette!

Quilting with the girls midweek
           still seems to take first place.
But now I plug my crock pot in
           for the meal that I must face.

I think about that little note,
　　　how some things you can't plan.
My love of quilting will never replace,
　　　my love for my well-fed man!

Thanks to my husband, Howard, of twenty seven years,
my biggest fan, well-fed and watered!

❈ The Label of Love ❈

She wrapped the quilt around the girl
And kissed her new born cheek.
Her heart was sad, eyes filled with tears,
This child she could not keep.

She had no means to raise a child.
She'd give her to another.
She wanted the best for her girl,
A home with a father and mother.

> The quilt had long ago been stitched
> By a woman across the land.
> She'd made it for an unborn child,
> Crafted with love by hand.

> The woman had a broken heart
> No child she could bear.
> They'd always dreamed of little ones,
> A loving home to share.

One day she took the quilt she'd made
And wrapped it up with care.
She sent it to the 'Moms in Need',
She sent it with a prayer.

It held a little label
With a rose like the yellow sun.
"You are loved, you are special,
You are my chosen one."

The young girl said her last goodbye
As they took her child away.
"I love you, little one," she cried,
"And each day I will pray,

That God will give you parents,
Who will say when day is done,
You are loved, you are special,
You are my chosen one."

46

The two could barely comprehend
The blessing come their way.
The child that they'd been longing for
Was coming home today.

They signed the papers, picked her up
And held her in their arms.
She smiled at them, their hearts were won
As they gave in to her charms.

                    With renewed hope, and lightened hearts
                        With plans of a life to build,
                    The nurse cried, "Wait!" She turned around,
                        And came back with the quilt.

                        The mother gently touched the cloth
                        And said, "How can this be?
                        I know each heart and flower and square,
                            For this was made by me."

47

Naomi Pearson

The quilt that she had given away
To be used by an unknown friend,
Had comforted one, embraced a child,
Now was given back again.

God's ways are sometimes not the ways
I'd choose in life for me.
Today I hold the precious quilt
That Mom passed on to me.

I thank Him for the mother
Who gave my life it's start.
And for the mom who loved me
As a child of her heart.

Like the quilt, God had a plan
Before life had begun.
I am loved, I am special,
I am their chosen one.

Dedicated to my birth mother, Dolores, who gave me life,
and to my mother, Olive Klaiber, who taught me how to live it.

48

*My birthmom, Dolores Allin and I
enjoying a quilt show together.*

Naomi Pearson

⊠ These Things I Value ⊠

"I've met a girl to be my bride,
And share the life I've built."
I knew that this event required,
A homemade wedding quilt.

I chose the colours carefully,
Worked late into the night.
I wanted it to bring them joy.
It had to be just right.

I added border, the binding was,
Invisibly stitched in place.
I looked forward to the special spot,
My wedding quilt would grace.

They moved away and bought a house,
That they could call their own.
They invited us to visit them,
And share their brand new home.

We arrived, then after lunch,
I subtly looked around.
I checked their bed, the living room,
But no quilt could be found.

I checked the den, under the beds,
Behind the closet door,
My husband finally grabbed my arm,
What was I looking for?

"I cannot find the quilt I made,
The wedding gift I'd planned."
I could see that as he rolled his eyes,
He did not understand.

Obviously my new daughter,
Did not appreciate my gift.
I was hurt, then very annoyed,
This slight could cause a rift.

Naomi Pearson

We were shown to our room that night,
The quilt was on our bed.
With chocolates on our pillow,
A little note that said,

I value this quilt you made so much,
It's used for special guests.
Thank you for your son, your love,
The time you both invest.

I sat and ran my hand once more,
Across their wedding quilt.
My husband's laughter shook the bed.
I was consumed by guilt.

I prayed that God would help me more,
When differences occurred,
To love my son, the girl he chose,
And show I value her.

For my friend, as she learns to be the best mother-in-law
to the wonderful girl who is now her daughter.

52

from
the
hands
with
heart

◼ A Legacy ◼

I guide her choice in colour,
But allow it to be hers.
We use straight lines in random form,
Over points on edge or curves.
I show her how to press with care,
Stand the iron as she ends her task.
I try to listen carefully,
To the questions that she will ask.
I show her how to run the thread,
To the needle of her machine.
I teach her how to 'frog stitch',
When she makes a crooked seam.
I love the days when my granddaughter,
Comes to sew with me.
I treasure this time beyond our quilt.
I'm leaving a legacy.

*To Fran, an example of the kind of grandmother
I hope to be.*

Naomi Pearson

❄ Better Than This ❄

What could be better than a carload of quilters
Ready to hit the road?
What could be better than spending a day
At the local quilting show?

What could be better than scooping a sale
At the little quilt shop in Lacombe?
What could be better than sharing a meal
With food even better than home?

What could be better than viewing the beauty
Of quilts hanging row upon row?
What could be better than inspiring new projects
That this year I simply must sew?

What could be better than listening to demos
And finding new methods to glean?
What could be better than sitting and trying
The latest in sewing machines?

What could be better than tickets drawn
Til the grand prize is all that remains?
The only thing better than this day in April
Is hearing them call my name!

Naomi Pearson

⊞ By Hand ⊞

I love to sew with my machine
　　　　to feel its sense of power.
To complete a quilting project
　　　　in the minimum of hours.
I love to find a pattern book
　　　　with projects by the score.
I whip them up on my machine
　　　　and then I look for more.

I cross-hatch using masking tape,
　　　　no measuring for me.
I stitch the ditch and stipple
　　　　in curves and maple leaves.
One day I saw a floral group
　　　　within a diagonal band.
The style just intrigued me,
　　　　'til I saw the 'stitch by hand'.

"By hand," I said, and shook my head,
      "this one would not go fast."
My friend said, "Hey expand your world,
      why, you should take a class!"
Now things by hand were always
      something I chose to avoid,
Assured the teacher was the best,
      you know she is Jean Boyd!

I went to class that Friday morn,
      a sense of apprehension,
I liked her samples and her style,
      she gave detailed attention.
She showed us how to pick and choose
      the colours that would go,
How you basted round the edge
      of paper as you sewed.

This wasn't bad and, actually,
        quickly passed the time.
After basting flowers and leaves,
        it was appliqué time.
Straight up and down and over one,
        careful not to show,
The stitches all along the edge,
        catch just the tiny fold.

I threaded up my needle,
        to match my flower of red.
I pulled it through but somehow,
        I had lost the fine silk thread.
I tied a knot, and set my jaw,
        a new determined mind.
I sewed the flower and to my awe,
        no stitches I could find.

Jean said the class was over,
>> they all let out a moan,
But I was on a roll and knew,
>> I'd finish them at home.
I quilt no more on my machine,
>> to hand stitch is my plight.
Today I stitched a leaf of black,
>> With thread of snowy white!

After taking my first hand appliqué class
with Jean Boyd,
and loving the challenge of
hidden stitches.

61

Naomi Pearson

▣ Determination ▣

I will not quilt today,
I've determined in my heart.
My home needs my attention,
I don't know where to start.

My underwear needs washing,
My windows need a shine.
The bathrooms need some Pinesol,
The kitchen needs some time.

Now what is that I see upon
My crumb infested floor?
A spool of thread is tightly jammed
Beneath a cupboard door.

I dig it out and know that
I should put it right away.
I'll go up to my sewing room,
I will not quilt today.

I go up to my brand new room
To put my thread away.
But notice things up here are in
A state of disarray.

While I'm here I think
That I will colour code my thread.
It won't take long and then I'll go
Right back and make the bed.

My thread arranged by colours,
So I turn to go,
I will not quilt today,
I will not press, I will not sew.

But while I'm there I notice
A new quilter's magazine.
New patterns I could build
From my extensive stash of green.

I look into my closet
Where I know my stash is stored.
And see a bulge behind my high tech
Folding pressing board.

I tug the board and past my head
My red stash hits the floor.
I need to organize this stuff,
I know I could do more.

I pull the bins, all ten of them,
Begin to sort and fold,
The florals here, the colours there,
Keep new and oust the old.

Rainbows of fabric are now spread,
Some losers and some winners.
I hear our truck and realize
That hubby's home for dinner.

I start to cram my stash in drawers,
My hair gets a quick spray.
I run downstairs to heat some soup,
I will not quilt today.

I stack the dishes in the sink
And go to dust the ledge,
But see my little sewing shears
Beside the can of Pledge.

I run the stairs, knowing this
Will take no time at all.
I see my stash upon my floor,
In fact, it's wall to wall.

I roll my eyes and pick my way
Through stash to scissor drawer.
I pull too hard and spill all of
the contents on the floor.

Naomi Pearson

Scissors, needles, bobbins, pins,
More thread, some small beads too.
I think that while I am right here,
Why not sort a few?

I take my special cushion,
That one that suits me best,
Poke red heads - north, yellow - south,
Green/blue, east and west.

I stand up and admire my work
But bump against a shelf.
I dump my entire button box
Right on top of myself.

I sort each one by colour
In jars put safe away,
I will not press, I will not sew,
I will not quilt today.

My sewing room is spic and span,
Each item in its place.
I feel as I look around
It's a productive day.

My underwear needs washing,
My windows need a shine,
The bathrooms need some Pinesol,
The kitchen needs some time.

When my man walks in the door,
I can truly say,
"I love you, dear, you'd never guess,
I did not quilt today."

*Written after two weeks
of 'power quilting' getting ready for
Valley of the Quilts, our bi-annual quilt show
in Drayton Valley, Alberta.*

Naomi Pearson

❋ Handmade With Love ❋

She sits
in the dim night,
her work lighted
with only
a kerosene lamp,
exhausted from a day
that demanded
all she had to give.
Winter is coming
and with it
the bite of cold.
She stitches carefully,
guarding the only needle she owns,
in fabric fashioned from
the precious cloth surrounding
the sugar,
flour,
and salt
from the previous
winter supplies.

She smiles,
knowing the
new quilt
would enfold
the little life
that is growing
within her.
She crafts her quilt
with love.

She sits in the corner
of her log cabin,
amazed by
the steady rhythm
of the treadle
beneath her feet.
She appreciates
the single bulb
casting a warm glow
of light
for her work.

69

She fashions her quilt
from the flannels
and calicos of
worn garments
that carry
the promise
of a little longer life,
from areas not
yet worn through.
She anticipates
the afternoons ahead,
when the ladies will meet
and hand stitch
together the new quilt
that will encourage
the latest couple
that have chosen to marry.
She crafts her
quilt with love.

She sits
in her new sewing room,
enjoying
the new cutting table
and rotary cutter.
She goes
to her stash
that she has purchased
from the latest
shop hop,
that included
ten stores.
She chooses patterns
from her
extensive
selection
of books
and magazines.

Her lighting
is carefully designed
to resemble daylight.
Her machine
can embroider
with the touch
of a button,
yet she chooses
to create by hand
from colours
carefully chosen
to resemble
days gone by.
She smiles,
knowing her grandmother
will appreciate
the warmth
of the lap quilt.
She crafts her quilt
with love.

 I Quilt

What do you do? My friend explains
       the business that she's built.
When they turn to me, I smile
       and simply say to them, "I quilt."

We live in a day when speed
       is the gauge we use to get things done.
From fast food to speedy lubes,
       no time for anything or anyone.

We use our cells and bank at drive thru,
       your machine calls mine.
In our high tech world we have lost the gift,
       now we no longer have... time.

But choosing fabric quickly
       would be a financial disgrace.
I have chosen a way of life,
       which requires a slower pace.

My design is selected after
        searching through magazines,
That I drink with a cup of hot chai tea,
        in a china cup laced with cream.

I carefully lay out my fabric,
        measure not one but two,
Using my ruler and rotary blade,
        slowly cut all layers through.

I try to make sure that my quarter-inch seams,
        are accurate, even and tight.
My points are sharp, my patterns match,
        when laid from left to right.

No one stands and watches over me
        waiting to use their clout.
For I've learned if I let myself hurry,
        I just have to rip it out.

So I stitch and chat with my quilting friends
and create a thing of beauty,
That is often fashioned for someone I love
with no sense of obliging duty.

By firelight, under my ott light,
I finish my quilt by hand.
The pressures of the rushing world
seem but grains of sand.

Instead of the hustle of our high tech world
which could fill my life with guilt,
I put on music, share some tea with a friend
and stitching with love, "I quilt."

Naomi Pearson

 Judy's Quilt

"I'm going to have a baby, Mom,"
My daughter said to me.
I could not wait to tell my friends
At my Wednesday quilting bee.

I'd watched the quilts created
By excited grammas-to-be,
And finally it was time for one
To be handcrafted by me.

Perfect squares of white and blue
Would frame a fuzzy bear.
I bought fabric for the border
To be hand stitched with care.

I worked when I could on the little quilt,
But life got in the way.
Illness, winters in the south,
And then, retirement day!

A brand new home with much less yard,
Friends and family,
Somehow the demands of life
Left not much time for me.

Today the bear quilt is complete
It's wrapped and finally done.
And it will make the perfect gift,
For my new GREAT grandson.

Naomi Pearson

▦ My Friend ▦

She might have been a doctor,
Or maybe a receptionist,
Instead she is a quilter,
A recovering perfectionist.

She has every quilting gadget,
One could possibly desire.
Working Mondays cutting fabric,
So more stash she can acquire.

Her pattern book collection,
Is a library of its own.
Her friends all benefit from that,
For she will freely loan.

She always presses every seam,
And measures more than once.
She brings baking, chocolate covered fruit,
And often shares her lunch.

When a job needs doing well,
She is the first one that we ask,
For you know detailed attention,
Will be given to any task.

She is generous and caring,
Her zest, it has no end.
Life's problems just seem smaller,
When I'm quilting with my friend.

To Twyla,
you bless me.

Naomi Pearson

▓ One More Quilt ▓

We've raised all of our children,
Three girls and one fine boy,
And thank our Father daily,
For the overwhelming joy.
How each one has enriched our lives,
In their independent way,
They've married, left our nest,
We're ready for grand babes!

It seemed to take forever for,
That first baby to come,
But suddenly the day arrived,
Our daughter had a son.
I formed a quilt with cross-stitch,
With his name and then his weight.
Our next girl said, "Keep stitching,"
They'd just got their due date.

I barely got the bunnies done,
When another call came through.
"Don't put your needle down,"
Our youngest child was having a baby too!
Our son then called to say that I,
Had better make another.
Then our oldest called to say our first,
Was going to have a brother!

Five new babes in two years,
Five quilts to stitch by hand,
Sometimes overwhelmed by them,
Beyond my wildest plans.
I was tired of the pattern,
I had chosen for my babes.
Two alike is fine but five,
Might send me to my grave!

Today we both embraced our girl,
They lost their little one.
God chose to take their baby home,
Life had barely begun.
My quilts are almost finished,
And tonight I ask you, "Lord,
Give my child peace, if it's in Your plan,
I'd love to make one more."

*My friend's girl was blessed with twins
in April 2005*

❖ Paper Piecing ❖

I learned a new technique this week,
In my ongoing quilting caper.
I learned to make small squares, sharp points,
By piecing them with paper.

The pieces were so tiny,
They could not be cut and sewn,
Putting patterns onto paper,
Designs were neatly woven.

The only problem that I had,
Was the paper I should choose,
Tissue tore too easily,
Newsprint, too hard to use.

Computer paper was too stiff,
Dulled needles one by one.
Someone said the best to use,
From a doctor's examination.

Naomi Pearson

I went to the local pharmacy,
To see what I could buy,
But they said, "Doctors Only"
From a medical supply.

I was so disappointed,
Then I came up with a plan.
I made a quick appointment,
For a medical exam.

I answered all his questions,
"What brings you here today?"
I brushed against the paper,
That I knew they'd throw away.

The examination over,
He said, "You may get dressed."
The paper that I'd sat upon,
I stuffed into my vest.

I stitched through the remaining week,
I happily traced and cut.
It wasn't long before the,
perfect paper was used up.

Committed to the cause,
I knew what I must do.
I have an appointment on Friday,
With a new doctor at two!

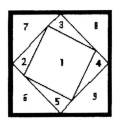

❈ Pink! ❈

PINK!
Such a … girl colour.
The call was for pink.
One block,
any style,
any shade,
one size,
PINK!
The blocks began to arrive.
pinwheels,
log cabins,
carefully hand appliquéd,
a rose,
a tulip,
a pansy,
All
PINK!
such a … girl colour.

86

A shooting star,
a square on point,
a hand stitched
English garden,
all the same size,
in one hundred
variations of
PINK!
The squares came from
all across the country.
They were joined,
squared,
sandwiched,
quilted,
some by skilled
hand stitches,
some by those
who had mastered their machines,
a great mass of
PINK!
such a... girl colour.

Today I tucked
the quilt around
my friend,
a gift from a guild
in a town
she had never been to.
"I'm so glad it's pink," she said,
as she gently
touched the empty spot
where her breast had been.
"I have never
needed more
to feel like
a girl!"

❖ The Block of the Month ❖

"Come join our team, make a block each month,"
The lettering said on the sign,
A whole quilt top for the low, low price
Of $11.99.

Surely this was a printing error,
I could not believe my eyes.
How could twelve whole blocks be made
For $11.99?

I touched the fabric, then took the paper,
And carefully checked the terms.
If I paid the fee, and came each month,
A new block I would earn.

The fabric was in jewel tones,
With leaves and vines entwined.
I'd never get a finer deal
Than $11.99!

I paid my dues, could hardly wait,
For the first block made by me.
But I had forgotten the previous plans,
I had in Kamloops, B.C.!

I had missed day one, to get my block,
I had to pay a fine,
But it didn't matter and I happily paid,
$11.99.

November came, the block complete,
I waited for Saturday to come.
Then I remembered the appointment I'd made,
Of the meeting with my son.

I could not let him down, I knew,
I'd miss just one more time.
To get my block I'd have to pay,
$11.99!

December I was determined,
That I would not miss the day.
Somehow my block did not get done,
And so I had to pay.

That first Saturday in January,
I was proud that I'd remembered.
Unfortunately, I brought the block,
That was completed for November.

In February, Mom bought tickets,
So we'd spend some skating time,
I sighed and once again I paid,
$11.99!

In March I was the speaker at,
A women's spring retreat.
In April I was sick in bed,
With a cold I couldn't beat.

By May, I knew a block of the month
Was sometimes not so great
I had paid $11.99
Not one time, but eight!

In June I arrived on time,
But this time in a snit,
I'd cut something wrong and therefore,
I had to buy another kit.

91

Naomi Pearson

In July I arranged my life,
The first Saturday would be free,
But because of a holiday it was now,
The second one they'd meet.

In August we were in the hills,
Spending some quality time.
I faithfully picked up my late new block,
Paid $11.99.

September came and somehow I knew,
My block of the month would be late.
The quilt top that seemed too good to be true,
Cost $143.88!

❀ The Cult ❀

"My wife has joined a cult," he said.
No case on which to build,
For all I'd done was choose to join
The local quilter's guild.

A cult consumes your thoughts and mind,
And causes obsessive devotion.
The guild only meets once a month
No support then for his notion.

I went to my first meeting
Which started with Sew and Share,
A private quilt show, I had no idea
There were so many projects out there.

The girls were friendly, tips were great,
The meeting ended too soon,
Then one gal said, "Come sew with us,
On Wednesday afternoons."

93

I packed my machine and little bag
With a tiny project to sew.
By the end of the day, I had fresh ideas
And three new UFO's.

I woke up Thursday morning
With patterns in my head.
I should cook and clean, but then I thought
I'd go fabric shopping instead.

Armed with bolts of fabric
Inspired by the guild,
I sewed Friday, Saturday, Sunday,
Monday and Tuesday were filled.

I could hide my hoard of fabric
If I always paid with cash.
My shelves were overflowing
With my multicolored stash.

Underneath my mattress,
Hidden 'neath the dirty clothes,
In a box labelled feminine care,
In there he'd never go.

Behind some books, rolled up tight,
Among my underwear,
I was out of control, but frankly,
I really didn't care.

My husband, he would smile at me
With slightly veiled pity,
So I didn't dare admit that I'd
Just joined the planning committee.

I knew I was in trouble,
When he held me and kissed my cheek.
I kissed him back but in my mind,
I was designing flying geese.

95

There were classes on first Saturdays,
On Tuesdays we could meet.
Of course, I planned to go and enjoy,
My first quilter's retreat.

A cult consumes your heart and soul,
Obsesses you day and night.
"Honey, I hate to say it,
But this time you could be right!"

A cult without a leader,
Would soon be a non-event.
Next year I am running,
For quilt guild president!

. . . sew glad we're friends.

*Celebrating my 50th birthday
with some of the Wednesday girls.*

97

Naomi Pearson

▓ The Puzzle Bag ▓

It's easy, eight fat quarters,
Four to match per side.
I knew that this was going to be,
The easiest pattern I'd tried.

You fussy cut that little print,
They all go the same way.
Then you follow the diagram,
See how the pattern is laid.

Start with one, add two and three,
Cut the corner off of four.
I cut it wrong, took a piece from a friend,
And had to cut some more.

It didn't match so I had to take,
The time to head downtown.
I finally found the perfect match,
After making many rounds.

I cut my pieces carefully,
Well, as close as they could be,
For I'd forgot my glasses
And I simply couldn't see.

I made a trip to the dollar store,
Bought a new pair for three bucks,
Came back and sewed my blocks together
With no wrinkles, slips, or tucks.

The teacher gave instructions
That the simplest could understand,
But I have a terrible habit of thinking,
I have a better plan.

She said be sure to start right here
And continue round and round.
I started there, went up not down,
A new best friend I found.

99

Naomi Pearson

His name is Jack the ripper
And the frog stitch I perfected.
I picked each thread so my mistakes
Would never be detected.

I had to start all over
But I finally got it done.
The day was now half over
And I'd completed my side one!

Side two I did so carefully,
Fussy squares in row three.
As I put it together, two birds stood on end,
One sideways, one flew free

I ripped them out, put them back in order,
This time all facing the top.
I was determined this Saturday project
Was not going to be a flop.

I tacked on handles, right sides together,
And then began to sew.
I tried to turn it right side out
But did not leave a hole!

The frog stitch again, leaving a space,
I got it right this time.
My puzzle bag, with a few detours,
Turned out mighty fine.

I thought of gifts for my sisters,
As we chatted that night on the phone.
I thought, then sent them eight fat quarters,
And instructions to make their own!

Naomi Pearson

❇ The Shop Hop ❇

Our day began in Edmonton,
My husband at the wheel.
We were on a holiday,
And my mind began to reel.

I had my paper carefully tucked,
In the side of the passenger door.
I had directions in my possession,
To every quilting store.

There were recipes and little quotes,
All neatly written down,
And directions to the fabric shops
Of every little town.

I longed to see each fabric shop,
So I bravely dared,
"Let's stop and see the 'Chicken Coop,'
While going past Mundare."

He didn't balk, but pulled right up,
Then sat back for a snooze.
Loving my shopping excursion, thought,
"What have I got to lose?"

"I'll drive," I smiled,
With plans to stop at the Vermilion mall.
I shopped first in another store,
Tucked in an old town hall.

He patiently did crosswords,
Or walked along the block,
Once in awhile he'd wander,
Into a local coffee shop.

It was now high noon and hunger,
Was something we couldn't avoid.
I found a bistro down the street,
From the quilting shop in Lloyd.

I made two great finds in Saskatoon,
My stash he never saw.
He raised an eyebrow when I found,
More quilt shops in Moose Jaw.

In Regina I found the perfect print,
A batik in Estevan.
This holiday I was seeing just,
How blessed I really am.

In Swift Current we stopped midday,
To fill the car with gas.
The quilt shop was across the street,
I added to my stash.

In Medicine Hat I had to call,
To find the store's location.
My hubby sighed but then complied,
As we were on vacation.

Not once did he say, "No,"
As I explored each treasure.
The value of such a wonderful man,
Is impossible to measure.

He never entered in the stores,
My search to interrupt,
But seemed content with a paper,
And coffee in his cup.

If I own a shop I know that I,
Will make a brand new rule.
A quilting shop should always be placed,
Next to a House of Tools.

Naomi Pearson

 The Sale of the Year

I could not believe my eyes,
As I read the garage sale ads.
Fabric by the bolt or piece,
In plains, calicos and plaids.

Patterns, notions, quilting books,
Dating back to '62,
I simply could not miss this sale,
What treasures to go through!

Wait a minute! This can't be right,
My excitement turned to stress.
For this garage sale of the year,
Was at my home address!

For my friend, Val, who made the mistake
of letting her husband see her stash!

◈ Today ◈

Never put off 'til tomorrow,
    What you can do today.
I've recently discovered that this,
    Is not the quilter's way.

My day was filled with household chores,
    That kept me on the go.
I cooked and cleaned and polished floors,
    But never had time to sew.

Mom was coming for a visit,
    I looked forward to the day,
And wanted to surprise her,
    With a new quilt on display.

I knew I had to take control,
    Of all the household chores,
So I made a 'today list' –
    A list of five – no more.

Wipe the fridge, not clean it,
      Sweep the floor, not wash,
Do not become distracted,
      By the trash that I could toss.

Clean the downstairs bathroom,
      Dust the living room,
Take out meat for supper,
      Be sewing my quilt by noon.

I did not get distracted,
      When chores got in my way,
I started a 'tomorrow list',
      For what I couldn't do today.

I never cleaned a closet,
       Unless it was one of five.
My quilting time, no longer,
       Something I had to deny.

The colours were just perfect,
       For the bed in my spare room.
The quilt was almost finished,
       And Mom would be here soon.

My today list is longer,
       Now the quilt is on display.
I can't put it on tomorrow's list,
       For Mom arrives today!

❂ War and Piece at the Border ❂

My UFO is almost done.
Flying geese are all in order.
The only thing that's left is to
Choose colours for my border.

I have a pink and chartreuse blue,
Two narrow lines, I'll build.
Wait, I think I'll get opinions
From my good friends at the guild.

I lay it on the sandwich board,
Imagine my delight,
When they oohed and aahed and told me
That my colours were just right.

One shook her head, turned around
Dug deep into her pack.
"Replace the blue, make it wider,
You can use my piece of black."

"Black!" another friend,
Now snorted to my left,
"You'd wreck the look," she turned my quilt,
"I think the blue is best."

"Blue's okay," another said,
"The pattern is so bold,
That centre block needs setting off,
With a little band of gold."

I began to get opinions
Coming by the score.
Then someone suggested that
We go down to the store,

And borrow several bolts,
A number of ideas,
To find the perfect colour,
The border sure to please.

111

Our arms were laden down,
With bolts from which to choose,
Purples, reds, olive green,
And even a chartreuse.

Make it wide! Make it narrow!
Please use three instead!
All of this for one small quilt,
To lie upon a bed!

My UFO is now complete,
It makes my room look new.
My borders are two narrow strips
Of pink and chartreuse blue!

Guild friends are always wonderful with
suggestions and second opinions.
They are never offended if you ignore them.

112

Naomi Pearson

🏵 Wednesday at the Guild 🏵

I spend my Wednesdays stitching
        with our local quilting guild.
I'm learning so much more
        than which new quilt to build.

I've learned that fat quarters
        have nothing to do with weight.
You alphabetize your crayons,
        if you want to keep them straight.

To sandwich does not involve
        any meat or cheese or bread,
But tape and pins and helpful hands
        to help you get ahead.

A UFO is not
        the local spaceship in the sky,
But a project started, set aside,
        more fabric now to buy.

A stash is not the chocolate,
   I have tucked down in the drawer,
But fabric hidden through my house,
   in cans, and bins, and doors.

To stipple does not really mean
   new ceilings in my home,
But don the gloves, and gently cause,
   my thread to curve and roam.

To crosshatch does not involve
   some chicks or geese or ducks.
The quarter inch and walking foot,
   are a definite quilter's must.

Cinnamon buns and cookies,
   fruit with chocolate dip,
Calories don't count on Wednesday,
   Is the quilter's dieting tip.

Naomi Pearson

So now when Tuesday comes,
I anticipate its end.
I know that Wednesday's coming,
I'll be sewing with my friends.

I'll pack my stash, my UFO,
and load up my machine.
I'll see new ideas, helpful hints,
tips that I can glean.

Now if I could only change
the one disturbing sight.
My family still wants supper
every Wednesday night!

For Hearts and Hands Quilt Guild
Drayton Valley, Alberta

116

Naomi Pearson

▦ Wednesday Weigh-in ▦

We quilt together Wednesdays,
Not all we do that day.
We try to build each other up,
Before we sew, we weigh.

We bought a fancy scale.
It weighs us so precise.
We cannot cry, "This scale is out!"
You weigh not once, but thrice.

We record our new weight weekly
With paper and a pen,
Pay a tooney when you have gained,
Take out when you lose ten.

We skip breakfast for the weigh in,
We know at coffee break,
There'll be goodies for indulgence,
Fruit for the faithful's sake.

118

There are some who lose a pound a week,
Some who just seem weaker.
Some who strip their clothing off,
And turn in to a streaker!

Now if I could just include,
An exercise regime,
Where I could burn up fat and flab,
Sewing at my machine.

Balancing on my exercise ball,
I roll myself around.
I ended ripping out my seam,
While seated on the ground.

I tried to swing my feet,
They were used for my controls.
I tried to hold my tummy in
And make my shoulders roll.

Naomi Pearson

I even brought my DVD,
Placed it near my quilt,
I watched my new Pilates tape,
Began to feel less guilt.

I plugged in my new headset,
And stitched to the upbeat,
Of an invigorating workout,
I could almost feel the heat.

So this week I watched and listened,
As I sewed every day.
I don't understand as I weighed in,
The numbers said,
"You pay!"

from the

Peace

of

the

pieces

Naomi Pearson

◼ The Colours of My Today ◼

I stand before the bolts of cloth,
In kaleidoscopic array.
I wonder how I can possibly capture,
The colours of my today.

How do you stitch a sunrise,
With its brilliant golden glow?
How do you recreate the glistening,
Of freshly fallen snow?

The northern lights as their racing colours,
Crackle across the sky,
The crystal emerald of a glacier lake,
Boiling streams rushing by.

Majestic peaks that change and shift,
From clouds that shadow the sun,
The scarlet hues of sunset,
As it signals day is done.

The starlit sky, iridescent moon,
A brilliance to light my way,
The cloth in my hand, but a dull reflection,
Of the colours of my today.

❈ Seasons ❈

Spring!
The world awakens
after the cold of winter.
Geese return, robins bring promise,
the brook breaks free,
tulips cautiously poke their heads
through the dormant soil.
My heart swells
as I scan the horizon
and see the fresh green
in the new buds
of the forest stretching
as far as my eye can see.
The soft pussy willow
makes me smile.
There is promise.
There is new life.

Summer!
The foliage is full
and the flowers
cause a splash of colour.
The beauty of the mountains
take my breath away.
The rushing glacial streams
give a welcome relief
from the relentless
heat of the day.
The campfire welcomes friends
and feels like a hug
as we share
laughter and stories.
The cool of the evening
refreshes.
There is fullness of life.

Autumn!
The colours soften,
decay hints of closure,
The bounty of another harvest.
The overwhelming riot of colour
as the leaves
turn crimson and gold,
a blanket of beauty.
The gathering of geese
as they know the warmth has ceased.
They find each other
and enjoy the strength of
companionship as they head south.
The crunch of leaves under feet
as you walk
under the hazy blue sky .
There is a feel in the air,
a fragrance.
There is calmness of life.

Winter!
A crisp kiss
that takes your breath away,
A silence as the world you know
slips under a coverlet of snow.
There is a glow
as the moon casts its shadow.
There is delight
as morning hoar frost
embraces each branch
of the leafless trees,
turning the ordinary
into the extraordinary.
There is awe
as the northern lights
crackle and dance
in a myriad of brilliance
against the night sky.
There is tranqulity of life.

My heart is overwhelmed
enjoying each season
as You have made it.
I cry, "Thank you, God."
If I pause,
I hear the still, small voice,
"You're welcome, my child,
I did it for you."

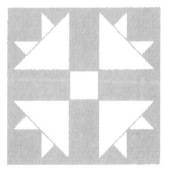

◢ The Quilt Designed for Me ◢

What would my quilt look like,
That was Master designed for me?
Would I understand the pattern,
That was woven intricately?

Would I recognize the colours,
The value and the hue,
Representing all experiences
I'd already travelled through?

Would I think the design odd,
With stars and gentle curves?
Would I understand the meaning
When I had no spoken word?

Could I trust the Master's touch,
His kaleidoscopic choice?
Would my life quilt clearly show,
That I had listened to His voice?

I'm sure there'd be some somber tones,
For times that I had failed.
Deep blues for times I'd conquered
And for easy times I'd sailed.

A splash of red for all the times,
I'd done things with pizzazz,
And grey for times my heart would break,
The times I'd made Him sad.

The patterns would be planned
And lined up in a row,
Then suddenly a seeming flaw –
A jagged line would go.

A curve and then some flying geese,
A diamond in a square,
Why would the Master mix up
Such designs as I saw there?

I wanted to take the quilt from Him,
To put it in my hand.
It was hard when I could not see
His carefully chosen plan.

But, who better than the Master
So to Him I will release.
From what I would have tossed,
He's made
A quilted masterpiece.

The Lord God is with you.
He is mighty to save.
He will take great delight in you.
He will quiet you with His love.
He will rejoice over you with singing.
Zephaniah 3:17

131

Acknowledgements

Thank you to my family, who have patiently listened as I have been writing. Thank you, Howard. You are my greatest encourager, not only with this book, but in every area of my life.

Thank you to Iris Tuftin, who tirelessly walked me through the workings of a book and spent many hours reading and editing. You have become a valued friend in the time we have spent together. I have much to learn from you. Thank you, Twyla Gardiner, for your creative imput and eye for detail. You are a treasured friend.

Thank you to the Wednesday girls. You have opened a whole new world to me through your friendship and unlimited quilting knowledge. Your stories have made me laugh and have given me much material for this book. You have always encouraged me to find the best in the gifts God has given me. I look forward to many years learning and sharing together.

Thank you to my mom for allowing me to try so many different things over the years. Your quiet encouragment has made me versatile. Thank you for all the beautiful gifts from the sewing machine. You are one of my best friends.

Thank you to my birth mom, Dolores, for the gift of life. Your belief in my abilities has made this book possible. Thank you for the gift of laughter and perseverence. I look forward to creating together.

Thank you to my God, the Peace of the pieces. I am thankful for my faith in a God who does not change. It is His world that we try to capture in the finite avenue of fabric art. I am overwhelmed with the peace I find from Him in the middle of the pieces of life.

Now may the Lord of peace himself give you peace at all
times and in every way. The Lord be with all of you.
2 Thessalonians 3:16

about the author

Naomi comes from Rocky Rapids, Alberta, a small hamlet five miles north of Drayton Valley. She lives on an acreage with her newly-retired school principal husband (the retirement is new, not the husband).

Howard serves on the school board and wonders how he ever had time to work as he fills his life with projects (none of them on Naomi's honey-do list).

Naomi is retired from teaching private voice, being a director of worship at her local church, and coaching drama. She is an inspirational women's retreat speaker sharing from God's Word and her gift of music.

Howard and Naomi enjoy their empty nest but feel complete when the family is home for a visit. They enjoy mountain camping with their horses and friends.

Naomi loves scrapbooking, cardmaking, and, of course, quilting. She has a home business with The Pampered Chef to help pay for her hobby habits.

Naomi is best known for her easy laughter and unique sense of humor.

from the author

I would love to hear from you.
My email is pearson_studio@yahoo.ca
or mail
Box 106, Rocky Rapids, Alberta
Canada
T0E1Z0

Books can be ordered at the above with
a cheque or money order.

Peace by Piece Selections CD
available.